Now Serving:

Memories
For
Lunch

Cover Photo:
captured through the eyes of Max
Bad Poetry:
etched upon the heart of Madison Blue

This book is dedicated to the loving memory of my parents Theodis and Mary Fisher. They taught me well. My heart holds their voices, individually and collectively. They blessed me with the knowing that love never takes more than it gives. Even more they gave me the will too try, the support too fail and the courage too succeed.

Thank you seems such a small sentiment to offer to those that gave this project and I endless support coupled with encouragement. Both, when I wanted it and especially in those moments when I did not. I have shoved this book aside more times than I can remember only to have someone revisit it with an inquiry or compliment. In those instances I was once again drawn to her pages.

Writing has always been the well that quenches my thirst and I need to drink from it often. Fortunately the prevailing wisdom that lights our path blessed me with a family that nurtured my needs. I can never thank my family enough for having always known that and always, always encouraging it. Though I will not list each of you by name, please know my heart is honored to wear each of your names indelibly on the role call of those that I love.

There are a host of friends that read what I write, and too my surprise they even like it. To each of them I say thank you.

This book bears the whispering of my soul. When my soul was weighted with emptiness four very special friends gave me strength, encouragement, determination and the light of possibility. To Judy Martens, to Eunice "Mert" Murray, to Cathy Hernandez and to Phyllis Lunsford I am forever in your debt. Thank you!

Lastly I have to thank Paulette (Max) Saffle, I will forever consider myself lucky for having shared time with you. My heart is the better for it. The thought of the you that I knew will forever linger in my writing.

Madison Blue

When love first called my name I raced into its wind with my heart wide open and my eyes ablaze with wonder. Though we never stumbled over what we felt, I did, no we did wake up to find our hearts in pieces. The glimmer of forever that we hoped our love could touch drowned in the mire of a silent goodbye neither of us wanted. Afterwards I found myself turning the pages of my emotions without allowing time to see if my feelings cared enough to whisper. Even now I do not know the wrong or the right of that.

What I do know is that along the way I looked, I watched and was often surprised by love's intent. I also developed a passion for bad poetry. Possibly because nothing embraces words more than a heart dancing on the brink of falling or one waiting to land. Anyway the pages that follow are written from the things I have seen hearts find the courage to do.

I invite you too walk around in my memories, hopefully at journey's end you will have found it a walk worth taking. I have not learned all of love's teaching, but maybe the lessons of yesterday will blend gently with my tomorrows.

Madison Blue

Memories For Lunch

For your dining pleasure:

The Road To Love

I was drowning in a reflective pool
beneath a watershed of pain
certain that fate had claimed my heart
in it's losing game
as the undertow yanked me down
for the very last time
I knew love was a dream
that would never be mine
yesterday felt so far away
and tomorrow was out of my reach
I was mired in the ebb and flow
on a eroding beach
walking aimlessly through the darkness
without even a prayer
until your heart touched mine
and showed me how to care
the look in your eyes
kept saying that this was really meant to be
you opened your life without hesitation
and sent your love to rescue me
showed me an open window to forever
with a warning that it was temporary and very rare
but if I wanted you promised
that the road to love was ours to share
then you took me by the hand
and stole my breath with your kiss
and I knew there was nothing I didn't have
that I would ever miss
the nearness of you
allured me to be free and wild
because you loved me with the strength of a woman

and the imagination of a child
the tenderness of your soothing touch
reached me across time and space
restored color to my rainbow
and put the smile back on my face

The Camelot Syndrome

When Romeo kissed Juliet
the taste of death brought him pain
your heart walked away from mine
and I felt the very same
as I sit here trying to understand
what, why and how it all went so wrong
wondering if I will every greet another day
without feeling absolutely alone
yesterday lost in your love
the whole world felt right
I could think of looking into your eyes
and count the stars that fill the night
as I dreamed of holding you close
feeling your body pressed against mine
I never thought we were part of the Camelot
Syndrome
perfection running out of time
or that my love would be pouring from a battered
heart
spewing out destiny's bittersweet sorrow
still hoping that your need will call to me
across some faraway forgotten tomorrow.

A Poet and the Lady in Waiting

Once I saw the summer of my dreams
wilt slowly beneath the winter kill
everything I envisioned love to be
was discolored by all I could not feel
paradise somehow misplaced my heart
while forever turned an empty page
leaving tomorrow to wear yesterday's memories
as hope crumbled on an abandoned stage
Until the lady in waiting brought the sun to me
bathe me in the soft warmth of it's light
held me tenderly in the quiet of her love
eased the loneliness from a empty night
now her presence floods me like the echo of a
whaler's song
my heart dances carefree to the sound of her voice
the thought of her touch gentles my restlessness
I am anchored by omniscient choice
Even when the treacherous storms of life
rain down on me again
I know I'll find her kindness gently waiting
to befriend me at rainbow's end
because when a lost poet's soul
stumbles through an unwritten scene
the words, the rhyme, the music of someone's
laughter
is the magic to heal a broken dream.

Newport, The Rain And Mrs. What's Her Name

Hidden in the closet of mind beneath the cobwebs and dust
I ran across some old memories that creaked from years of rust.
Some were as painful to remember, as they were to live in their original inception
Once or twice I was shocked to recall that I was capable of such deception.
Other's time had gentled and only the pleasantries remain
Like the week I spent in Rhode Island in lust with Newport, the rain and Mrs. what's her name.
We met at a friend of a friend's dinner party, some sort of formal affair
Black tie, evening gowns in a room full of pretty people, I was completely out of my element there.
Several times throughout the evening we were introduced by mutual friends
 I was always impressed by her polite hellos and the delicate way she squeezed my hands.
I wasn't sure she even recognized me from one introduction to the next
But as my friends and I were leaving she casually invited me back to her house for sex.
I considered her offer flattering even though I was certain it was made in jest
Yet, somehow later that evening I found myself at her home as per her request.
We spoke of my school and sorority;
she implored me to make the best of my college days
She also told me to always remember

that pleasure is the key to life's satiric maze.
As she talked I could think of nothing
but the fit and feel of the evening gown she wore
I watched in awe as she allowed it
 to tumble ever so slowly to the floor.
The only thing that she was left wearing
 was that come-hither look in her eyes
 Newport, the rain and Mrs. what's her name
 filled my week with highs.

Stolen Moments

We keep sharing stolen moments
pictures lost in time
you tell me the secrets of your life
I speak of the heartaches that is mine
is that really all there is to this
two ships passing briefly through the same light
or are we two hearts in desperation
struggling to make it through another lonely night
is this made easier because we are strangers
and I wouldn't know your face in a crowd
or would my heart instinctively know yours
and be recalcitrant in it's need to call your name out
loud
perhaps it's being able to share the truth, yet still hold
on to the shadows
that enhances these meteoric interludes in which we
partake
or could we have once danced under the same
moonlight
and this is a romantic apparition that neither of us can
forsake
yet, maybe we just enjoy stolen moments
pictures lost in time
simply playing an innocent child's game
of you show me yours and I'll show you mine.

She Didn't Know How To Stop Loving You

Today I heard the familiar sound of another heart
breaking
a soul suddenly cast adrift on the ever changing
wind.
One fell so easily out of love
whilst the other stayed so obviously in.
Now, her colored Polaroid dreams of forever
have turned to nightmares in black and white
as she tries diligently to solve the puzzle
of what went wrong and make it right.
She called you once to often
desperately needing the comfort of your voice
only the words you spat out in anger
made moving on her only choice..
When you told her you would no longer tolerate
these uninvited intrusions in your life
she thought the only solution left her
was a sink of hot water and the cold blade of a knife.
Alone in the bedroom
of the house the two of you once shared
she chose to walk the coward's road
leaving behind a note addressed to someone who
once cared.
Drenched in her blood was the pillow
that for a time held your head
the room you two once bathed with passion
rang silent with the sounds of dread.
She wrote she didn't know how to stop loving you
how to make her yearning for you subside
she couldn't pretend that it was over

her feelings were just to strong to hide.
So, she found her letting go place
by slashing a knife across her wrists.
Ending her words of guilt to you
with the sting of a bloody kiss.
Now, she has changed your life forever
your guilt has bound you to her grave
though her love wasn't strong enough to hold you
her death has made you it's slave.
But, it's time for you to stop punishing yourself
and know her words were not true
the reason she chose to take her life
wasn't because she didn't know how to stop loving
you.
Really being in love with someone
means giving them the space they need to breathe
not wrapping your weakness around them
fulfilling your own selfish needs.
Today I heard the familiar sound of another heart
breaking
a soul suddenly cast adrift on the ever changing
wind.
One fell so easily out of love
while the other needs time to help her heart mend.

The Mirror Says

For the better part of a year
        I've stood quietly at you side
nursing you through more pain
        than anyone should abide

Shouldering every tear
        you've felt the need to cry
watching her use your love
        then leave you with a lie

 Listening to you make excuses
        for the promises she neglects to keep
talking you through the lonely nights
        when you're too worried to sleep

 Trying desperately
        not to let my feelings interfere
wishing I had the strength
        not to want to be here

Silently praying that someday
        you will open your eyes and see
there's someone dying to love you.
        the mirror says it's me.

Winter With You

Beneath a white lace blanket
hidden from view
our love is waiting
wanting to be made new

Lost in your delicate smile
animated by your touch
I can think of nothing
I ever wanted so much

Your eyes scream their message
their urgency is truly felt
I feel my hands trembling
as my icy heart begins to melt

Inflamed is my undeniable desire
for it is still only you that I need
Please allow me to fulfill you
I'll await your answer before I believe.

Forever

Would it be easier for you, if I were to just disappear?
Then could you put away your memories of me and
erase all of our years?
No, I don't think so, you will never be able to forget
the richness of our passion or how we loved without
regret.
You always said, " I made you flow as fast as a raging
river,
that just thinking of lying beside me made your entire
body quiver."
It still amazes me how our aching need could flood us
with desire
the touch, the taste, the smell of you would set my
soul on fire.
We were so in love you said, " Your heartbeat spelled
out my name. "
Every now and then, when I think of us, mine still
does the same.
Was it the sameness of our sex or the difference in the
color of our skin
that made you abandon our love and bring about it's
end?
We were dancing on the edge of perfection, so very
right for one another
that even though we stop making love we will never
stop being lovers.
I would gladly disappear if I thought it would truly
bring you peace
but this aching lustful hunger we share will never
really cease.

We may never touch again or find our way back together
but the one thing I'm most certain of is that our love will live forever.

The Note Upon The Fireplace

It was twenty years ago today that I ran home so
excited
to the love I spent all day anticipating
I could hardly wait to taste your lips
feel the love flow through your fingertips
drown in the passion I'd been awaiting

But the note upon the fireplace said please go have a
happy life
the time I had for loving you has all gone
maybe you'll understand some day
and realize that I had to go away
please know the love we shared wasn't wrong

I sat down on the floor and cried as the tears fell from
my eyes
I wished the love I felt would turn to hate
I was angrier than I had ever been
and the pain just kept crashing in
like a storm that renders the river's boundaries negate

I was empty inside ashamed that I didn't have more
pride
because the largest part of me was praying you'd
come back
still I was determined to get over you
bitterness would see me through
until forgetting you became a matter of fact

As I wiped the tears from my face I admitted my trust
in you had been misplaced
and I sealed myself off to you forever
I vowed I would never repeat these same mistakes
I'd avoid love no matter what it takes
protecting my heart would be my only endeavor

I swore to myself that I was over you
and tried tirelessly to prove it true
even though I couldn't erase traces of you from my
mind
the faster I ran, the closer you seemed
I try to sleep and you'd steal into my dreams
no matter where I ran I couldn't leave you behind

Then your mother tracked me down one day told me
sometime ago you had passed away
the cancer you had been battling had robbed you of
your life
her words stole away my breath
you never once allowed me to see your strife

The tears streamed slowly from my eyes my head
spun with questions and whys
I could barely ascertain the words your mother spoke
she opened a letter from you and began to read
you wrote, please my darling don't you grieve
for the love we shared was my brightest hope

You were sorry you ran out of time said all your love
was forever mine
and that it was thoughts of me that had quieted all
your fears

you made me promise not to waste my life crying
because you said leaving me was harder for you than
dying
and to please think kindly of you in the coming years

It was twenty years ago today that I ran home so
excited
to the love I spent all day anticipating
I could hardly wait to taste your lips
feel the love flow through your fingertips
drown in the passion I'd been awaiting

But the note upon the fireplace said please go have a
happy life
the time I had for loving you has all gone
maybe you'll understand some day
and realize that I had to go away
please know the love we shared wasn't wrong.

if it's never my turn

if it's never my turn to hold you
        at least I held you in my dreams
I danced with you beneath the setting sun
        and enjoyed all of love's extremes

if it 's never my turn to kiss you
        at least I embraced you with a thought
I felt my heartbeat spell your name
        and shared the passion lovers have always
        sought

if it's never my turn to be with you
        at least I can think of us like lovers in a picture
        show
our destinies forever entwined
        so I never really have to let you go
if it's never my turn to feel you
        at least the hint of your touch made me believe
you dusted the hurt off my heart
        and gave it a future to conceive

so, if it's never my turn to lie beside you
        at least know I could not have wanted you
        more
you gave me a moment to remember
        gift wrapped in a love worth waiting for.

even if it is never my turn.

Again

You danced across my thoughts again
and I started to remember when
we were so alive with love
that I just knew,
tomorrow was only a breath away
and I would undoubtedly be spending mine with you
like t.v. lovers riding off into the setting sun
we would still be loving when the final scene was
done
Only someone forgot to say
that life could step in and take you away
and death can visit even when the loving is young
leaving behind an empty lover who needs two to be
one
trying to build a life after the living has gone
Unfortunately we were not the kind of lovers the
world celebrates
from time to time we felt the need to mask it away
from uneducated hate
mistakenly I mourned you the same
secreting away the wholeness of my pain
until,
you dance across my thoughts
again

Christmas Greens

In a world of broken spirit
from a sad and lonely heart
the will to love again
allows the misery to restart
I find I believe in laughter
the joys of yesterday
and everything I ever said to you
plus the words I didn't say
I should have held you close to me
loved away your pain
instead I watched you walk away
as the snow turned into rain
It makes me think of Christmas
the seasons of my youth
life and love where simpler then
gift wrapped in the colors of truth
The tree standing tall in my family's home
while the angel holds the light
as we bake cookies for Santa Claus
and sing O' Holy Night
The air smells of Christmas greens
adding fuel to fantasy
tonight I was visited by the ghost of love
and left wishing you here with me
In a world of broken spirit
from a sad and lonely heart
that still dreams of miracles
and the magic of snowflake art.

Merry Christmas

The Kidnapping

I woke up tired in Michigan
       in a hung over state of mind
in the arms of the lady
       I thought I wanted for all of time
Last night started out in anger
       but it rolled away with every mile
now I'm lying here watching her sleep
       being comforted by her familiar smile
Trying to understand how our way to love
       became such an un-solvable mystery
by sifting through the foggy haze in my head
       reviewing our recent history
Lately we've directed so much energy
       into hurting one another
that I wasn't at all certain
       we could stop long enough to be lovers
But here she is waking up in my arms
       with that look in her eyes that I miss
the one that says she will not allow her day to begin
       without first enjoying my kiss
We basked in each other's love for days
       thinking of nothing but the pleasure we
       engaged
until the talk of going home
       made us equally outraged
Her scenario of our romantic escapade
       was that I kidnapped her against her will
it didn't matter that she had shared the driving
       and it was her name worn by the hotel bill
Or that when I had offered to take her home
       she made the decision to stay

she just smiled in that way of hers
      and said she would not relive it that way
Because the man that she had been dating
      has ask her to be his bride
she had given him her reassurance
      that the oddity of our friendship is solely from
      my side
She talked endlessly about her wedding plans
      as I drove home in silence
wondering just what the price I would pay
      for this mistaken alliance
Parked in front of her house
      she kissed her fingers and pressed them to my
      cheek
promising with a smile
      we'd get together one evening later in the week
Only while we where leaving Michigan
      my heart finally bid hers good-bye
and as our love fell to the earth incomplete
      I was too relieved to cry

All I Know

I love her; she hurts me
why is love such a mystery
time has come to let her go
but I still want her and that 's all I know
when a poet writes there are no words she can't use
when a heart loves there is no glimmer of hope it
won't infuse
even pain can fuel love's flame
and a battered heart bears the shame
the one who clings to love's remains
often grows complacent by the wearing of the chains
and doesn't know her heart has been empowered
with a strength to survive that can't be deflowered
I love her; she hurts me
why is love such a mystery
time has come to let her go
but I still want her and that 's all I know
broken love makes a strong heart grieve
it's not always easy for the one who had to leave
love dies quiet like a summer's lawn
the darkest hour is always before the dawn
not all stars fade before the night reaches the morn
there's always hope love will somehow be reborn
a last chance waltzing somewhere in the wind
that two hearts can find separate places where love
does not end
I love her; she hurts me
why is love such a mystery
time has come to let her go
but I still want her and that's all I know

Her Ghost

Out of the stillness of my grief she animated my
dreams
patiently she nursed my sorrows like a river feeding a
stream
with her heart pressed against mine she re-ignited my
passion
wrapped in her tender embrace we returned pleasure
to fashion
the warm inviting fire in her eyes romanced my tired
soul
her sage caring and concern made my shattered heart
whole
she reached deep inside and halted my spiraling fall
and propped me up with her strength when life came
to call
she whispered to me softly when our room was
bathed in dusk
tantalized me with the sweet shadow dancing of our
womanly musk
time and again I tried to hold our magic in the cold
light of day
only to succumb to the familiar dread as it slowly
fades to gray
but every night I found her ghost alive and waiting
in our bed
her kiss would bring our love to life; if only in my
head.

two women, one love

there were two women who shared one love
it was nothing they were looking for
it whispered through an open door
these women, these women shared that love

there were two women who shared one song
they knew from very the start
they were singing to each others heart
these women, these woman shared that song

there were two women who shared one kiss
the fire when lips first met
was a flame neither could forget
these women, these women shared that kiss

there were two women who shared one night
their passion made their souls dance
entangled with the taste of romance
these women, these women shared that night

there were two women who shared one ride
when it ended there was nothing left to say
they fell in love but for only one day
these women, these women shared that ride

there were two women who shared one love
it was nothing they were looking for
it whispered through an open door
these women, these women shared that love

Fairy Tale Hell

We were everything that we wanted us to be
but we couldn't see it with open eyes
Yet you're still trying to hold on to the dream
while me the dreamer dies
Love called our names from a distance
we both recognized her gentle voice
being the infallible humans we are
we decided she made the wrong choice
What we once bespokenly thought of as love
was really friendship hiding behind destiny's veil
everything we felt was just a mirage
we were temporarily lost in fairy tale hell
Whispering words of forever
like star crossed lover's somewhere in time
our hearts shared a common rhythm
like poetry metered in the same rhyme
Now we are trying to find the reason
for emotions we can't quite comprehend
christening this bond we share in the name of
friendship
because neither of us can let it end
When the conversation turns to sharing our life with
others
jealousy is as pullulate as can be
because I still need to hear you say, I love you
as much as you need these same words from me
So not much has really changed between us
even the dying dreamer will survive
when I close my eyes and hear you say it
I begin to believe we can keep this dream alive.

Woman To Woman

I looked back and wondered about things in our past
searching for answers to questions that may be best
unasked.
What really happen to the friendship we both craved?
Did it really have to end or could it have been saved?

Was it laden with boundaries to vast to reach across?
Or   perhaps throwing caution to the wind was an ill-
fated toss?
Were you the victim or the perpetuator of my
unbridled lust?
Because even now I'm not sure how we went from we
to us.

Either your kissing me or my caressing you
unleashed a hunger
that we were both to weak to resist any longer.
Though as I recall, we did make an honest attempt
maybe our exhausted efforts make us both exempt.

Woman to woman you lead me wantonly to your bed
though not for sex, you made sweet love to me
instead.
Passion thundered between us, our desire raged until
it blazed
we could lose ourselves so completely in one another,
that I would wake up dazed.

Without ever having to ask we just always seem to
know

the right touch, the right rhythms, the right time to go
slow.
We were more than mere music, we were a
symphony to raptures delight.
At times I was certain my heart would burst when
you were ravishing me to new heights.

Our never being lovers would have been a sin of
omission
so why couldn't our friendship survive the transition?
Was I so busy loving you that I didn't help to
subjugate your fears?
When the demons of doubt were chasing you should I
have held you near?

Maybe my entry into your life was an inescapable
intrusion
and no matter what we did we would have reached
this inevitable conclusion.
Because you were trying to pattern your dance to
compliment the lyrics of my song
when what you truly thought you wanted was
husband, hearth and home.

But, every now and then when one of us weakens and
dials the numbers on the phone
I hear the seeds of doubt in your voice wondering if
you may not have been wrong.
You say almost nightly I steal into your dreams
even when making love to your husband, you thirst
for the heat of our passion and desire to drown in our
steam.

You yearn for the erotic shades of ecstasy, the tears of
exulted bliss, the emotional imagery we always
summon
to enthrall the sweet, gentle, tender intimacies we
shared loving woman to woman.
Walking away from the drama of our relationship
was like flying in hurricanes winds
the need is to raw, to eager for us to stop being lovers
and still be friends.

The Park

I saw you in the park today
I stood there watching you play
with your new friend

My mind kept searching for reasons
my heart kept rerunning the seasons
before your new friend

I heard myself saying this really can't be
this morning she made love with me
now she's romancing her new friend

You gave her the smile you said was mine
the world around me stumbled in time
watching you and your new friend

I stood there so deeply in love with you
wishing one and one and one equal two
listening to you laugh with your new friend

I stayed long after watching you leave
because my heart and soul refused to believe
how happy you were with your new friend

Finally I wondered home through the night and rain
one look into your eyes and I knew yours was the
greater pain
because it's not a victimless sin it's your new friend
I held you and promised that everything would be
fine

no one's to blame that your heart has left mine
for you new friend

Our tears spoke all the words that neither had the
strength to say
we kissed good-bye and I watched you walk away
with your new friend

A Heart That Is Haunted

Wistfully I've been trying to force love
from a heart that is haunted
a heart brimming with images so vivid
that their grasp is undaunted.
When I look into a mirror I'm so coupled
that my reflection isn't alone
she's poised in the background
seductively summoning me home.
Only there's no home to run to
we destroyed it with our rage
for her being in love is like trying to live life
from inside a gilded cage.
As for me I need at least the hint of commitment
a basis on which to build a foundation
although every minute without her
is an eternity lost in damnation.
Over the years we have both fell victim
to our aborted attempts at compromise
forged from a desperate desire to be together
that we both agreed to terms we despise.
Only to discover
once the overwhelming passion is relieved
that we are no closer
to the conducive harmony we sought to achieve
And once again in a bed
steeped with sexual gratification
we engage each other over fences
built from hurtful proliferation.
Until we find ourselves repeating
the same good-byes neither of us wanted
and yet again I'm wistfully trying to force love
from a heart that is haunted

Silent Love

Welcome to the festive cabaret
that has recently became what was once my life
just ignore the faceless clock on the wall
it's a souvenir, a remembrance of a long ago strife
it's droning is my timeless admonition
and whispers loudly to my exasperated heart
cautioning me against letting go
before I even give love a chance to start
only this time there is a difference
I have to know the sweetness of your embrace
just thinking of you makes me know
falling in love with you is not the same as falling from
grace
the mere thought of touching you
has colorized my passions that long ago turned pale
conceiving mentally the thrill of our kiss
has me standing here breathlessly waiting to exhale
there is not much I can say
to reassure you that this is not a mistake
just place your hand in mine
my love will never let your heart break.

Your Letter

Quite sometime has passed since our last goodbye
I hoped by now you had realized we were never
meant to be
only today in my mail I found your tear stained letter
full of remnants of memories that are so faded I can
barely see
you said you are still buying my favorite coffee
the one I love to savor with the Wall Street Journal in
bed
last night you ordered my choices from the menu of
our restaurant
then came home and rotated my pillow to keep the
cool side against my head
you're still buying Bazooka Bubblegum and saving
me your red m&ms
your freezer is stocked with Haagen-Dazs chocolate,
chocolate chip
because in your heart you are certain that what we
shared
was far more than a temporarily port of love's ghost
ship
you swear your heartbeat is measured by the meters
of my breath
that your perfect moment is still the one owed by my
kiss
and that everyday the sun rises in your life without
me
is another day lost to despair, emptiness and wasted
being remiss
sadly you signed your letter from a heart that is still
quietly waiting

desperately needing to stumble fromthe darkness and
into the light
only there is nothing I want more than for you to find
that
but mine is not the love that can make your world
right.

Her Daddy's Little Girl

Thoughts of yesterdays tugged heavy on her
heartstrings
and left her standing on the wrong side of the door
wishing her past back into her future
yearning for a love that's been lost forevermore
basking in the warmth and comfort of their life
together
she envisioned them growing old in each other's arms
only weakness deflowered their timeless innocence
and society's bigotry separated them from love's
charms
parting sent her racing back into painful darkness
to the oblique closet of an inhospitable world
searching for the tender mercies of her childhood
blanketed in the security of being her daddy's little
girl
hiding in solace from the truth that she knows is her
trying to unlearn the lessons that reality sang out in
1977
when she crawled into a augur back seat
and lost her virginity trying to climb the stairway to
heaven
through her silent prayers she counted every salty
teardrop
knowing that this was not the love she was born to
make
finally she found the voice to tell a young man's
passion
that their venture to sex was a sad mistake
she was so afraid love was a road she would never
travel

until happiness beckoned to her in a gentle woman's
smile
the two of them shared a rightness
that never goes out of style
but somewhere between the love and the laughter
family discord and the world chipped away at her
dreams
as daddy's little girl stood by in silence
the love she prayed for fell apart at the seams
now all that remains is some faded yesterdays
only she can still feel the kiss on her lips
of the gentle woman who's love once saved her
though it's no longer available for daddy's little girl
return trips

My Shirt

Although we've never laid my shirt out in the sand
or made that crazy kind of love
that only teenagers understand
there's a part of me,
deep in the heart of me
that has never belonged to anyone but you.

Although we've never danced beneath the moon
or had to flee your mother's house
because she just came home to soon
there's a smile that I remember
it was my very best September
when life finally brought me to you

Although we never bathed out in the summer rain
or stood high upon the edge of a cliff
shouting our love to a passing plane
there's a time I will always hold
when the best secrets had been told
I lay beside love and woke up with you.

Although we've never laid my shirt out in the sand
or made that crazy kind of love
that only teenagers understand
there's a part of me,
deep in the heart of me
that will forever wear your name.

From Your Bed of Roses

The air permeates with the fragrance of your perfume
halting visions of us together resume
I can almost feel your slender fingers ruffling the
pages of my mind
enticing me back to another place and time
apprehensively I find myself engrossed with you on
your bed of roses
hypnotized by the suggestiveness the sultry feel of
you proposes
knowing this is a night we two shouldn't share
but tempestuously my passion erupts with the touch
of your silky hair
drowning all my resistance in the effervescent pool of
my desire
impeding any process of thought except for those that
you inspire
until the look in your eyes reminds me of the truth
that I can't ignore
your love isn't mine to have, only to temporarily
explore
because as often as we have tried, we cannot out love
your pain
rigidly it stands between us like lightning slicing
through the rain
unfortunately we never cross the threshold where
punishment absolves my mistakes
and you can't find a way to give me your heart
without waiting for it to break
so once again from your bed of roses I must take my
leave

because I know pleasures of the body is all we will ever achieve.

The Love We Didn't Make

The winter wind's whistle blew the snow in off the
lake
as we stood on your balcony pondering the risk we
would take.
I was bound to my lover by the love I profess
his ring on your finger was the source of your
distress.
Yet, here we stood a breath away from kissing one
another
knowing that if we did, we could not resist becoming
lovers.
You took me by the hand and lead me back inside
from your touch I knew there was nothing left to
decide.
You put some music on and asked me for a dance
the movement of our bodies together had us both
entranced.
Then, Dan Folgelberg sang Hard to Say and all our
doubts were cleared
our chance for being lovers had come and
disappeared.
So we spent the evening talking as we watched the
snow blow in off the lake
in the morning we shared a coffee toast to the love we
didn't make.
Our paths crossed years later, you no longer wore his
ring
the love that I thought was forever, for her was just a
winter's fling.
Over lunch we laughed about the evening that we so
naively shared

the passion we sacrificed for two who wouldn't have
cared.
You said you ended it because he was not the man
you thought
his idea of giving love was the price of the gifts his
secretary bought
I told you that losing her was far less than devastating
we couldn't commit beyond sex without vacillating.
We joked about our conversation being more intimate
than having sex
how the friendship that grew between us that evening
was more than anyone would expect.
We spoke of how it still gives us pause to see the
snow blow in off the lake
and again we shared a coffee toast to the love we
didn't make.

The Last Detail

Last night lying in the arms of the woman who's love
eases my pains and quiets all my fears
my world came to a sudden stop, when your gentle
touch
caressed my mind and rewound all the absent years
I was so rich with the thought of you
the way we loved without a care
that I could feel, taste and touch you
even though it's not your bed I share
every right thing you ever did
every soft word you ever spoke
came crashing back into my heart again
as if it had never been broke
I can still remember every response of your body
right down to the last detail
like winds filling an empty sail
I still know the rhythm of your heartbeat
I hear it singing in my mind
I can't seem to stop my fingers
from using her body to trace your lines
even though it's her beneath me
it's the feel of you that I can't resist
my need for you is so raw, so ready
you're the benefactor of my greedy kiss
showered in the rain of our passion
it's your voice I hear screaming out my name
as I look into her face awashed with pleasure
I feign exhaustion to disguise the shame.

December 10th

I was young but she was even younger
the night we shared on destiny's trail
with a bottle of scotch and no thoughts of tomorrow
we checked into a Buffalo motel.
Something in my eyes made her believe I'd be gentle
something in her laugh made me need to prove it
true.
As she toasted the blizzard that had stranded us
together
I lifted my glass with a birthday wish for you.
My forlorn sentiments aroused her curiosity
and I answered honestly that you were someone I
don't know,
but that you and I fill in the blanks with great passion
during the odd moments when the angry and the
arguments are slow.
I told her when I kiss the small of your back
your entire body smiles
and that you have a funny way of crinkling your nose
when sexually displaying your womanly wiles.
I told her how I love the way you say my name
there this softness that floods your eyes
it strips all my pain away
and demands that the rest of me complies.
As she peeled off her jeans she kissed me
and promised tonight she would give me her very
best
but while she was pulling up the covers in Buffalo
I was in my car racing the storm west.

Elaine

She says she knows when I think of you
        she can read it in my eyes
She says she knows when I'm remembering too
        there's this smile that I can't disguise
So how do I go home and tell her
        today you called out my name
Your smile melted all the years away
        and made everything feel the same
I said you were as beautiful as ever
        still looking as if you stepped of the pages of a
        magazine
You laughed and teased me about finally becoming
fashionable
        now that the whole world is wearing cowboy
        boots and holey blue jeans
You asked if I remembered making love
        at the Indianapolis Museum of Modern Art
I reminded you of our grand passion
        when we snuck into the stockroom of Kmart
You brought my hands to your lips and kissed them
        just the way you use to do
For a moment, I was that girl again
        that would walk through the fires of hell to be
        with you
Every emotion you ever awoke in me
        was screaming out your name
So, how do I go home and not tell her
        I made love with you Elaine.

Terms of Endearment, Misspent Words

In a quiet moment on a pain ridden night
staring at life from the wrong side of a case of Bud
Light
praying for company desperate to be alone
thinking of love in nineties a computer, a modem and
a telephone
painting word pictures of awkward embraces,
treasured memories and childhood scars
trying to show a friend you've yet to meet
all the sides of who you really are
while cautiously losing your heart
across a crowded internet
hoping you're not foolishly poised on the brink of
lover's regret
believing her terms of endearment are more than
misspent words
knowing the things she whispered are the very words
your heart heard
making you want your love and your life to be the
fountain from which her desire feeds
wishing the tender touch you offer can truly fulfill all
of her needs
happily you lose your innocence to whispered I love
you(s) like lovers in a soft easy country song
believing her to be someone to love and her love
someplace to belong
only she couldn't share your dreams of forever
because her heart continues to wear someone else's
lust

there is no blame to be placed when someone finds
love is still waiting beneath the dust.
just allow your heart to remember her terms of
endearment were more than misspent words
and thank her for the things she said, because they
were offered with the love your heart heard.

Interloper's Vacation

Come lie beside me
and I will teach you how to fly
I will pay homage to your body
and soothed all your whys

My strength will be your anchor
as you comfort your denial
I will show you a world
where this lifestyle is viable

If you still need
I will hide in the shadows and even pretend
that we are not lovers
just the best of friends

My concern will be your safety net
as you discover who you are
allow me to be the stepping stone
you use to reach for your star

There's no need to make promises
besides I know that you are afraid
so I will shoulder the responsibilities
while you enjoy the comforts of my bed

Feel free to take from me
anything that you feel you need
only my heart is the one thing
that I will not easily concede

Because I have been fooled before
by other women whom have had me convinced
that their heart was mine to hold
while they paraded on both sides of the fence

Not that I want to burden you
with any of the fragmented embers from my past
I just refuse to me the emotional umbrella
to anymore relationship ash

Forgive me if this sounds accusatory
but these are facts not accusations
my intent is only to protect my heart
if this is a detour on an interloper's vacation

Ruth And Alice

Ruth and Alice met in ballet class
     when they were eight years old
Alice was shy, kept to herself
     while Ruth was outrageous bold
Alice was awkward couldn't do the dance steps
     Ruth learned to pirouette on her toes
Ruth was a leader, outshined everyone at their recital
     Alice stumbled and broke her nose
Ruth grew up loving jewelry and dresses
     entertaining her friends over tea
Alice loved horses, shagging fly balls
     the outdoors and stories of the sea
Still, they became best friends, caring for each other
     made staying together their life long plan
Sharing the future the good and bad times
     being there when the other needs a hand
On a ride through the park one starry evening
     Ruth comforted Alice with a kiss
It startled them both though they had to admit
     their feelings were to strong to dismiss
So ten years of friendship
     that they both truly treasured came to a rapid
     end
Because they were to fearful to even allow
     these feelings a chance to begin
Alice left town in hurry
     ran off early to school
Ruth married Thomas
     and tried to live her life within the rules
Over the years that followed
     they both tried never to remember

The thrill of a forbidden kiss
      shared one evening in a long ago December
But in the end it was that very memory
      of an unforgettable ride in the carriage
That finally gave Ruth the strength to walk away
      from an unfaithful husband and end a
      thankless marriage
Now, Ruth and Alice
      have been happy for years
Taking care of each other
      sharing both the laughter and the tears
So, today in that same park
      surrounded by family and friends
They decided to open their hearts
      and invite others in
They spoke of their love and their lives
      and exchanged bands of gold
Under a sign that read; Ruth and Alice met in ballet
class
      when they were eight years old

Something You Heard Oprah Say

Today she called me on the phone
as if the last twelve years were just gone
I had barely finished my hi
when I heard the tears she was trying not to cry
I couldn't believe she had called me this way
trying to tell me something she heard Oprah say
Talking as if our friendship survived our being lovers
Even though she pledged herself in marriage to another
Lord knows I know right from wrong
and some things are best just left alone
We should never take pleasure from someone else's pain
but here she is crying to me just the same
As if she didn't know, that I am a bridge that she has burned
a corner she came to and chose to turn
I'm not sure what she heard Oprah say
but she wasn't talking to her today
Not if it made her think of our time together
because that's behind me now and forever
Neither she nor Oprah was at my side
when the love that I had been living for died
I lost too much of myself in her, that I didn't get back
nothing she nor Oprah have to say will change any of that
But even so when I hung up the phone
I couldn't resist turning my television on
Only fate could have planned it this way
I was just in time to hear Oprah say
Words that made me think of us

how we lost our innocence to passion and lust
She said, "Some relationships can't just end, they need closure
though you blanket your emotions they're still raw from exposure."
Lord knows I know right from wrong
but I couldn't help but pick up the phone
I told my lover what I heard Oprah say
she said, "You'll have to work it out some way."
In her voice I heard this sad little smile
when she told me, "Sometimes years disappear like miles
Tomorrow leads back to yesterday confronting the same strife
I can't tell you what road to chose, after all it's your life
Maybe all the bridges behind you aren't burned
maybe you both read the page but neither of you turned
I'm not sure what it is you must do
follow your heart and I will be waiting for you"
For the first time ever, she hung up without a word of good-bye
she rung my doorbell before I could find out why
Our instincts told us she did not belong inside,
so I grabbed my coat and we went for a ride
An old song on the radio took me back to days of her and I
the look on her face said it hadn't passed her by
As much as there was different, some things hadn't changed
but I was still surprised she had our destination prearranged

Waiting on her to unlock the door it crossed my mind
to leave
as if she knew what I was thinking, she caught hold of
my sleeve
As I followed her into the room I thought Lord help
me please
when I look at this woman I still get weak at the knees
Right then all I could think of was the taste of her kiss
and I wondered if I tried would she even resist
She got us beers she had chilling on ice
I thought what a fool I'd be to lose this woman twice
A voice kept warning me to be careful for the price I
might pay
could be the very one, I woke up for today
She kept me off balance with her questions
asking them as if I was still her possession
She said she would love to thrill me with her touch
only she was afraid I would take it to mean to much
She told me she had two little girls that still need their
mother
so all she had to offer was today, there would never
be another
I watched the pain in her eyes as I listened to the
words she spoke
for the first time I realized, mine was not the only
heart broke
I wanted to lie beside her, comfort her all through the
night
tell her stories like I use to and make everything all
right
But Lord knows I know right from wrong
and we were both someplace that we didn't belong
Looking back at memories that can't be revived

the time for our being just friends has not yet arrived
For the love between us is a bridge, that could still be
cross
only neither of us is prepared to pay the full cost
On the drive home I kept thinking about the words
we heard Oprah say
the truth of them that brought us together for a day
I wondered what Oprah would think if she knew
that I live a heartbeat away from falling back in love
with you

Ice Castles

Today a distant memory
whispered to my frozen heart
singing a song of loneliness
about lover's whom love apart
one pretends love has died,
portrays the charade of letting go
the other hides her love in someone new
praying it doesn't show
neither wants to believe in ice castles
because forever has fallen down
Cinderella never found her shoe,
and there's nothing as sad as a happy clown
Even though love shouts loudly
across a forsaken dream
their two hearts separately
can't help replaying the same scene
they are both afraid to stop,
and trust the love they share
to step into darkness
of their heart's truth or dare
to regain their belief in ice castles
the land where forever can be found
where stars shine in your lover's eyes
keeping your heart homeward bound.

My Moment of Weakness

The night summered romantically around us
as the stars danced regally in the sky
her eyes shined with the depth of diamonds
and whispered a smile that didn't need reasons why
Her skin relaxed against the warm refreshing air
as if it was waiting to know someone's touch
But she kept her movements metered
in an effort not to portray too much
Even so I could tell she was lonely
yet she was more alive than anyone I ever knew
her passion roared like flames in a wild fire
only in the heat of her desire my thoughts raced to
you
She asked if I had completely forgotten
how to throw caution to the wind
it would be a lie to say I wasn't tempted
but my heart would not let me begin
With tears of absolute sincerity she asked
if we could just share this one night
and opened her arms with promises of passion
that would caress morning's first light
I stood there listening as she reminded me
that no one was waiting for me at home
but even so in my moment of weakness
my heart spoke your name and our love held strong.

Love Lied

We started off softly barely touching hands
you spoke quietly to my heart made us the best of
friends
You calmed me tenderly invited me to your bed
painted my passion with your colors filled me full of
dreams to replace the dread

I was awed by your gentleness overwhelmed by your
sense of right
when letters was our only correspondences your
words chase the loneliness from an empty night
Only now I know a different you one who spends
time in someone else's arms
thinking you can hide the truth by blinding me with
your charms

As if I could forget it was your voice I heard when
love lied
left me standing outside myself trying to convince my
heart it hasn't died
I have yet to know a moment when I feel as if I'm not
drowning in the pain
or trying to keep the hurt from shading what we
shared with disdain.

Love lied.

McEwen Street

A memory of you came drifting through
on the notes of what you use to be our song
before I could reach and turn the station
my mind was already gone.
Back to the foot of McEwen Street
back to where our love was first born
back to where we use to dance and romance
and fan the flames of desire into the early hours of the
morn.
Now I'm thinking of how you use to were my
sweaters
I haven't thought of that in a very long time
but I remember how a trace of your perfume would
linger
and I could sense the feel of your flesh against mine.
And once again we would be slow dancing
our bodies embraced by the light of the moon
you would be singing the words softly in my ear
to whatever song we had just chosen to be our tune.
We'd make love and smoke one last cigarette
you'd lay your head on my shoulder while I was
driving you home
with your hand possessively clutching my thigh
I finally knew how good it felt to belong.
Back to the foot of McEwen Street
back to where our love was first born
back to where we use to dance and romance
and fan the flames of desire into the early hours of the
morn.

Yesterday's Jeans, Stale Beer And Cigarettes

Here I am lost again
> waking up in someone else's morning
the pain rushing around in my head
> isn't my only warning
that I spent yet another evening
> trying not to love you
I wish I could remember her name
> so that I could wake her and offer my regrets
as I slip into yesterday's jeans
> smelling of stale beer and cigarettes
I really need to face the fact
> that you no longer love me
then maybe I could stop looking for you
> in the passion of someone else's bed
start to heal my broken heart
> stop looking behind and focus on what's ahead
and never have to spend another evening
> trying not to love you
no more vacant mornings
> of hangovers and nameless regrets
slipping into yesterday's jeans
> smelling of stale beer and cigarettes
if I could only admit
> that you no longer love me

Memories For Lunch

Far too often I find that I dine
where memories for lunch is the chosen fare
once again I am forced to indulge
in the rendering of my heart's truth or dare.

Looking back at yesterdays
that inspired me too want so very much
to once again lose myself
in the stroke of a ex- lover's touch

Redefining who I think I have grown to be
by revisiting the thought of what we once shared
beckoning my heart to venture back
when ours souls was completely bared

Yet again I find that I dine
where memories for lunch is the chosen fare
once again I am forced to indulge
in the rendering of my heart's truth or dare.

The Mystery of Love

Cloaked in the mystery of love
the travesty of my life unfolds like a play
torn between two women
the desire to leave; the need to stay
her love is so new, so beguiling
it's taken my heart by storm
yet her love still floods me with magic
just the thought of her keeps me warm
her touch has awaken the part of me
that dances wildly on the wind
but every night in the arms of the other
I find my way back from where I have been
how can I say good-bye to either
when they both own my heart
and I need her and her
to keep my life from falling apart

No Strings

Here they sit in the floor of their apartment
calmly surfing through the last of their things
closing out a six year relationship
a love they lived with no strings

So many times she sought you out
with her heart weighing heavy in her hands
trying desperately to tell she needed you to be more
than a frequent lover and an occasional friend

She wanted your love to have purpose
she believed your emotions stronger than your fears
but every time she tried reaching out to you
you let her pleas fall upon deaf ears

You were selfish in your need to keep things simple
you enjoyed the pleasure without getting involved
the few times you acknowledged her distress
you took her to your bed and considered the problem
solved

Now it's you who's walking away feeling empty
the carefree one is suffering from a heavy heart
because the picture of you without her
is such a lonely portrait to impart

But, here you sit on the floor of your apartment
calmly surfing through the last of your things
choking on the memories of the love you foolishly
lost
trying to live a life with no strings

Reminiscing

Somewhere in the madness of another dream
        you sought me out once again.
Whispering to me of yesterday's forbidden
indulgence
        of friendships lost through lover's sins.
I'm not sure what you think we can accomplish
        by taking another stroll down memory lane
after all we have already admitted
        that some left over feelings still remain.
Reminiscing about our time together
        reliving mornings we woke up early to share.
Baring our naked souls over breakfast
        making love without pretense of savior fare.
Experiencing the intense richness of our pleasure
        by giving our all, leaving nothing saved
freeing ourselves completely, enabling our passions
to rant
        as raw and needy as they craved.
Only we were not brave enough to reach for
tomorrow
        we were unwilling to make the needed
        sacrifice
didn't have enough faith in ourselves
        to believe that we could build a lover's
        paradise.
You had to have the world's stamp of approval
        three tier cakes, taffeta dresses and lacy
        wedding veils
your mother's beaming acceptance
        Mr. and Mrs. gracing your mail.

Now that you have achieved the status you so
desperately wanted
        I'm sorry it's not all you thought it would be
but the happiness you're so recklessly seeking
        cannot be found here with me.
I want to promise myself to someone special
        and fill her with a love that will last
So, this is our last time for reminiscing
        never again will we reopen Pandora's box to
        our past.

Racing With The Devil

We were never the loving gentle souls
I seem to have created in my mind
Actually our love was bittersweet
the majority of the time
One of us was always running home
from someone else's bed
Yelling, cursing angry words
we never should have said
Breaking up may have been the only
civilized thing for us to do
But once we said our final good-bye
I fell deeper in love with you
You were no longer around
to chase away the shadows of the night
Which made me remember how you had opened my
darkest corners
and warmed them in your light
How could a couple
so bountiful with the potential for love
Know how to push all the right buttons
but consistently chose all the wrong times to shove
Until we finally destroyed all of the hope
that once solidified our dreams of forever
to the point where being separate
was preferable to being together
Only now I find myself racing with the devil
just trying to hold my place in line
Reeling from the bite of your memory
that always snags me from behind
Causing me to reflect on the way things might have
been

if we had not stumbled onto love so very young
Foolishly believing love could survive days fueled
with anger
and nights poisoned with the scent of a stranger's
lustful fun.

Ecstasy And Agony

No one will ever know, like I do
the pain and pleasure of loving you
I showered in the sweet gentle rain of your ecstasy
only to be swept under by the unyielding tide of your
agony
You've wrestled my emotions to the brink of insanity
then you calmed my spirit, quieted my soul and
restored my dignity
Once you told me, my love for you was no longer
required
when I asked you to explain you said you were just
too tired
You had spent the evening making love to someone
new
and if I weren't so selfish, I'd be happy for you
You were really disappointed and just couldn't
understand
why me the un-required lover wasn't acting like a
friend
I showered in the sweet gentle rain of your ecstasy
only to be swept under by the unyielding tide of your
agony
You've wrestled my emotions to the brink of insanity
then you calmed my spirit, quieted my soul and
restored my dignity
You called me to say that you had gotten engaged
I ran into at our favorite bar and you became enraged
Being without you was no longer my greatest fear
in fact someone new was now kissing away my tears
When I introduced you, you refused to use her name

instead you smoldered with anger and cast her looks
of disdain
You've wrestled my emotions to the brink of insanity
then you calmed my spirit, quieted my soul and
restored my dignity
You came to see me and you were so excited
being the first to share your news made me delighted
You laid my hand on your stomach to feel the life that
you bear
then you ask me to lie beside you and show you that I
still care
We made love all afternoon the way we use to do
then you called my lover and told her my heart still
belongs to you
And once again I showered in the sweet gentle rain of
your ecstasy
only to be swept under by the unyielding tide of your
agony

The Joke

this time the joke is on me
I showed her all that love should be
I honored ever word I spoke
build her bridge to me on promises never broke
I reached out to her when she was lonely in the night
tried to help make the wrongs in her world right
I answer every single time she calls
I'm there to brace her when she falls
my life will never be the same,
 because I played a loser's game
catching every tear she pretended to cry
ignoring the truth in order to dream of the lie
yet, she would rather settle for less
yearning for a dormant love to profess
words that will never offer anything more
than reliving the hell she barely survived before.

Farewell Dance To Loneliness

Lady, there's so much I need to say
before you take my heart that I offer you here today
Though I can't tell you trouble will never find us in
the coming years
I assure you I will always help you see the smile that's
hidden beyond the tears
There will never be any finger pointing or assigning
blame
and no two days that pass us by will I ever love you
the same
I promise your happiness will reflect in everything
that I do
I'll be your advisory, your confidant and I'll respect
your point of view
I will be as close as I can be and as distant as you need
there will never be anything you could ask of me that
I would not willingly concede
I promise to love you with all that I am and cherish
you with all that I know
but before our farewell dance to loneliness begins I
should tell you I'm not good at letting go
Though if the time ever comes and you find your
heart yearning for someone new
I only ask that you take a moment and teach me not
to love you
because it would sadden me if love ends and we can't
walk away friends
so now let's begin our farewell dance, my heart is in
your hands

An Unforgiving Heart

you were playing make believe
a grown up game of pretend
while I thought we were speaking words of love
that would never ever end
I didn't believe someone so opulent with honesty
could be telling empty lies
which is why your duplicity
came as such a appalling surprise
you possessed the kiss I wanted
to last a lifetime through
all the walls I architecturally contrived
came down because of you
you said that I had known far to much loneliness
danced to many dances with despair
because the people I erroneously trusted
could not see how much I truly care
inimitably your words massaged my soul
right from the very start
only now I'm standing alone in love
wishing that mine was an unforgiving heart
a heart that would not still welcome you back
and forget all the wrongs that you have done
because it can't stop singing your name
nor believing that you are the only one.

Forever Home

Loneliness echoes from behind closed doors of empty
rooms
memories I can't forget hold me in their vacuous
stares
as I sit and watch the tired misery of empty clothes
draped across the backs of abandoned chairs
I can't help but to wonder why and where
the love we lived for went so very wrong
When we were both damn certain we found our
forever home
in the arms of each other was where we belong
Even now I can still lose myself in the romantic
thought
of your hair falling seductively around my pillowcase
and it still fills me with passion to remember the
moonlight
dancing softly across the contours of your enchanting
face
Although the hurt gathered like dust on our feelings
there is not a moment we shared that I would not
miss
as the evening breeze whispers hauntingly through
my window
I am carried away by the memory of your sweet
tender kiss
Quietly I recall the lessons of a forgotten writer's
words
love always gives more than it ever takes
how much sadder I would be if my love had sat
dormant
fearing the thrill of the fall, terrified of the heartbreaks

I Can't Drink Myself In Love With You

Here I am pretending to watch a movie
        that we both know that I have already seen
Tonight you have that hungry look in your eyes
        and I know just what it means
You want me to come and join you
        taste the pleasures while we're chasing that
        thrill
As much as I hate hurting you
        I can no longer fake things I just don't feel
I never meant for any of this to happen
        you knew mine was a heart that you could not
        keep
But here I sit, while you are alone in our bed
        crying yourself to sleep
Now we're replaying this same scene nightly
        it's all so abstract and very unkind
I never should have agreed to stay
        when thoughts of leaving fill my mind
Your friends keep insisting that there is someone else
        they say I am not the type to sleep alone
Although you say you don't believe them
        I see it in your face everytime I come home
But, I not leaving for someone new that I found
        I'm searching for something that I have lost
I feel as if all the seasons have come and gone
        while I was buried beneath the frost
Lately I've been drinking way to much whiskey
        and more than my share of beer
Somewhere at the bottom of one of those bottles
        I was hoping to find away to stay here

But from the very beginning
    we always promised to be true
So now I must admit
    I can't drink myself in love with you

Passionate Mornings

Outside the rain is tapping
gently against my window pane
In every drop I hear it quietly
spelling out your name
Inside my closed heart
 is once again alive with desire
Ablaze with thoughts of endless nights
and passionate mornings that you inspire
I find myself yearning for sensuous words
that will stroke as tender as a lover's seductive touch
Enthralling you with the indulgence of an Epicurean
longing to find yourself lost in my amorous clutch
Waking up amazed by the love we made
refreshed by the warmth of our embrace and the need
to explore
With your lips lingering on mine
we will be reacquainted with the ecstasy we shared
the night before
This will be far more than either of us imagined
because we will be making love heart to heart
The magic of you will be shining in my eyes
with renewed wonder that thoughts of you impart

In the Pleasing Hush of Afternoon

In the pleasing hush of afternoon
our cupidity dances un-assuaged
echoing the mystique of morning's insatiable lust
and the memory of the ballet our bodies enraged
yet in the quiet aftermath of our episodic rapture
our passion spent, our bodies breathlessly tire
and still the mere thought of your touch
rekindles my need and inflames my desire
I am ravenous in my want of you
haunted by every kiss we have yet to share
only it is not my lustful intent that is speaking
my heart is burning bridges of lonely despair
yours is not a love I want to hold only for a moment
I could spend my life living in your eyes
your tender caress has awaken dreams that I had
forgotten
and all that I am has been revitalized
Now in the pleasing hush of afternoon
ablaze with the colors of eternal lights
can I tempt your heart to share my humble promise
of passionate mornings and endless nights
mine are not the words of misspent passion
painting romantic promulgates that quickly fade
away
for if life only offered me this once to lie beside you
it is where my heart would forever stay.

Whispering Out of Evening's Steam

Whispering out of the evening's steam everything I
ever wanted
found it's way back to my life smiling in your eyes
what I thought would be time lost to passion's hunger
became enchanted with the promise of an unexpected
surprise
Your kiss awaken a dream that I had stopped chasing
when I discovered her love no longer needed me
Passion became just a matter of inconvenience
until your desire embraced mine and set it free
In the tender ease of an unforgettable moment
I was reacquainted with a need I thought I had left
behind
but somewhere in the thrill of your touch
your heart craved it's initials permanently upon mine
Now I find my thoughts have begun romancing
forever
built around scenarios of living love with you
Sharing passionate mornings and endless nights
while enjoying each afternoon enough for two
Mine will never be the unblemished heart of
storybook hero
but I promise I will always love you the best I can
and though I am no one's knight in shining armor
you will find me a woman who cares enough to
understand

Endless Nights

My mind is stirred by the vision
of you quaintly standing there
your shirt causally unbuttoned
the seductive toss of your hair
I'm enthralled by the way your lips
slightly quivers as you strain to speak
besieged by an unyielding tide of hunger
as my passion climbs the summit of it's peak
Even though your words are ambiguous,
I can tell you're aching for my touch
to tame the beast of your resistance
in the silky exigency of my clutch
The thought of the sensation of your skin
pressed against mine has me hypnotized
I want so much for my dancing to fingers
to pirouette deep inside of you like I fantasize
Imbibe all of the juices
that your body express to quench my thirst
banquet on the array of your feast
as your screaming desires burst
Lavish you with the velveteen touch
of my tongue's long slow winding trail
inveigle with the alacrity
of your womanhood's gesticulating spell
Lose myself in the intoxicating sounds
that bespeak your body's vivacious delights
as we explore all the positions of our rapture
and surrender to the ecstasy of our endless nights

Come To Me

I saw a face in my mirror today
that I barely recognize
one filled with thoughts of you
that refreshed these tired eyes
there was a smile that wasn't weary
from hiding broken dreams
it wore a hint of playful energy
like a river feeds the streams
there was wealth in my laughter
that has been missing for quite sometime
if there was any sadness in this day
I can say honestly it was not mine
you have given me a moment
and even if it forever dances alone
whenever my soul needs healing
it is where I will go to feel at home
so if there is ever a time in your life
when things aren't the way you think ought to be
know that my world is always here
trust what's in my heart and come to me.

I Wish I Could Remember To Forget

I wish I could remember to forget
the velvet genius of your touch
the way you wrap your legs around me
when we're dancing in the throes of rapture's clutch
the gentle tickle of your teeth
as your tongue comes out to play
the fullness on your commanding kiss
that says more than words could ever say

I wish I could remember to forget
how you always know what is wrong
the way your love crawls inside me
and makes the weakness in me strong
how you softly scratch your initials
in the center of my back
and when struck by passion's thunder
you surrender your defensive pose and go on the
attack

I wish I could remember to forget
the thrill of your body lying next to mine
the way you whisper seductively in my ears
and overwhelm me with emotions to intense to define
how just looking at you
awakens my senses and flood me with desire
and the need to please you
recants any doubts that this love will ever tire

I wish I could remember to forget
the way it hurt to hear you say good-bye

how you looked at me with emptiness
as if everything we ever were was a lie
when you said you now needed to explore
some other woman's charms
taste the pleasures we once shared exclusively
while spending your evenings in her arms

I only wish I could remember to forget

The Goddess of Forever

Standing in the shadow of shattered love
facing another endless empty night
I pray to the Goddess of Forever
that someone is loving you right
Thrilling you with a touch that's unpredictable
awaking your fury that is sometimes remiss
flooding you with passion's fire
that breathes in the memory of a kiss
Answering the invitation to the dance
scribed by your insatiable need
caressing you with tender wonder
easing the ache of desire's ravenous greed
Standing in the shadow of a shattered love
facing another endless empty night
I pray to the Goddess of Forever
that someone is loving you right
Listening to those quiet little tears
you sometimes allow yourself to cry
hearing the I love you
hidden in your words of good-bye
And not allowing you to mask your emotions
behind a wall of uncertainty and mistrust
or letting you use ipsation to deny
that you need love to inspire lust.

Heart and Soul

I didn't know
        that life could be this good
you've touch me in a way,
        I never thought that anyone would
you brought laughter to my silence
        eased away all my pain
just the thought of you
        makes me know I will never be the same
you're the woman I've always dreamed of loving
        the one I didn't think I would ever find
although the way to you may be fraught with
difficulties
        I love you heart and soul, body and mind
I promise you this
        so please know these words are true
l will never
        abuse the privilege of loving you
there is no mistake that you could ever make
        that I can not find away to forgive
because a perfect world without you
        is a place that I would not care to live.

When We Are Two Old Ladies

When your step is a little slower,
your hair has all turned gray
the wrinkle cream you swore by
won't fade the lines away
I'll tell you of the beautiful young woman
that I look at you and see
if you doubt my words,
gaze into my eyes and I promise there she'll be

When you feel your dreams are all behind you,
you're leery about what the future holds
and you find yourself nodding in the middle of your
sentences,
forgetting what you've just been told
when sex has become a vague reminder
of something we use to do
I'll be lying beside you in front of the fire
still absolutely amazed by you

When your eyes are growing dim
and you tire way to quick
just reach out your hands
you will always find me as close as your fingertips
when everything we talk about
has a reference to by gone years
please trust the love I offer,
it will help vanquish all your fears

When we are two old ladies
closing out our day from our favorite chair

you will know your love is everything I want to do
again
and just how much I truly care
I will never be able to thank you for restoring my
belief in happily ever after
or for teaching me that fairy tales really do come true
but I can honestly tell you there has never been a
storybook princess
loved by anyone half as much as I love you.

In The Heart of Someone Kind

We strolled knowingly outside the circle
tangoed uninhibited into the unfettered range
the very first time we touched
I felt the whole world change

We've challenged those that have branded us
and judged our love immoral and against God's will
by having the courage to face our critics
and not hide behind friendship or some other codicil

You've taught me just how outrageous loving can be
when it's wrapped in the arms of comfort, honesty
and trust
I've also learned that it sometimes takes passionate
anger
to build the bridge between anguish and lust

Every night that you have laid beside me
I've felt my eagle soar
but, I especially love those mornings
when I've made your lion roar

Yesterday we were certain
our destinies were eternally entwined
today you say there are dreams beyond the horizon
that you need to leave me to find

I know I could convince you not to go
if I spoke to you of the perils of unforeseen danger
but using fear to make you stay

could destroy our love and turn us into strangers

And so, I say farewell my darling
I sincerely hope that you find
everything that you are searching for
in the heart of someone kind

She Loves Me More

Her sadness made me wonder
Her smile inflamed my desire
Her tears soften my granite heart
Her touch set my soul on fire

She gave me her love unconditionally
She sacrificed herself to fulfill my needs
She answered every time I called
She surrendered to my insatiable greed

Overlooked all my short comings
Offered me a shoulder on which to cry
Forgave my transgressions
Stayed when I didn't care enough to lie

I used her love like a weapon against her
Held her accountable for every mistake she ever
made
Bantered her past before her
Allowed her guilt to be a reminder that her debt was
unpaid

Every time I think her love has reached it's limits
because I've opened the wounds enough for the
misery to pour
She opens her heart a little wider
and finds away to love me more

Separately

This evening greeted me with the despair
of breaking up ravishing the air
Two people I care about called separately
to say they were no longer a pair
Somehow they had lost each other
between the anger and the " I love yous " that went
unsaid
now parting seems preferable
to sleeping separately in the same bed
Only I remember watching Amber fall in love with
Cindy
the very first time she touched her with her eyes
I was there to witness Cindy's heart lead her to
Amber
like Polaris guiding the shepherds through the night
skies
Yet here we are this evening
I'm the last one left in their relationship
trying to be the friend they both need
as love slips through their fingertips
wishing that I could make them see
that their road is meant to be together and not apart
because they can still touch the love they share
if they would only stop and listen with their hearts.

Unclaimed Love

All the lies have been
        told all the secrets sold
                I accept my guilt without proof
Loving me brought you pain
        for that I am to blame
                nothing stand as naked as the truth

I just could not resist
        the innocence of your kiss
                and I greedily hungered for more
I should have warned you from the start,
        not to trust me with your heart
                I've stumbled down that road before

I was too busy getting you in bed
        to say the things that needed said
                my burning desire was in command
I was blinded by my lust
        when I made you promises of us
                I beseech you to try and understand

It was never my intent
        that you be hurt when our passion was spent
        `   I only wanted to set this need in us free
you surrendered more than mere pleasure
        you entrusted me with your best treasure
                now all your tears belong to me

Because it frighten me to discover
        that I was your very first lover

the responsibility was more than I could
bare
so, instead of holding you in my arms
and protecting you from harm
I treated you as if I didn't care

Every single time you cried upon my shoulder
it reminded me that this wasn't really over
that a piece of my soul would always be
left behind
It was the bitter price I pay
for not having the courage to stay
and claim the heart that had captured
mine

Heather,

If I had a lifetime long and every other day stood still
there still wouldn't be enough time to tell you all that
I feel
for to simply say that I love you is far far less than a
start
because what I feel for you is like an undiscovered art
You helped me touch the sunshine you bathe me in
the rain
you laid down beside me and you took away my pain
showed me sound in silence how darkness bares a
light
now I love the stars to fondly to be fearful of the night
you took me to the mountains introduced me to a lake
now I know true beauty and it takes my breath away
You gave me the best of you asked little in return
only to share in the joy I felt when new things are
being learned
I watched you find yourself and lose yourself in
dreams
like a bird in flight you took direction from the
streams
so, I'd like to take this time to thank you again for all
that you did
and to tell you though it ended you life your love
taught me how to live.

One More Moment In The Sun

I always thought, we would just walk away when it
stopped being fun
but you asked if I had time for one more moment in
the sun
You cajoled and flirted, you were ever so eager to be
accommodating
used your knowledge of my body to seduce me into
participating
The signals I sent you by accepting were
disconcertingly mixed
While you were making love; I was just having sex
 I never meant to hurt you nor am I telling you this
now to be cruel
neither did I intentionally try to make you feel the
fool
For me it was never a matter of forever only for
awhile
and I sincerely believed that when it was over we
would end it with a smile
I never said I love you, I never once said that I care
every single time I laid beside you I thought that you
wanted me there
For pleasures of the body not for reasons of the heart
but now the look in your eyes says I'm tearing you
apart
I don't know how to comfort you or how to take away
your pain away
when I ask you what you need from me
one more moment in the sun is what you say

This Woman

This woman may forget to send roses
        but I'll give you a kiss gift wrapped in a dream
and even when I'm stumbling over my words
        I will find a way to express what I mean
This woman may never serve a romantic dinner
        but I will bathe you gently in the moonlight
and I promise before our time is over
        you will hear I love you somewhere in the
        night
This woman may never think to invite you to forever
        and I may buy a baseball when you're
        expecting a ring
but darling I'll try to write you a tender love poem
        from the quiet truths you've taught my heart to
        sing
This woman may never mention the pleasing way
you fill my eyes
        or how you take my breath like the ebb and
        flow of the tide
but that is only because I'm touched by all that you
are
        and I'm thrilled that your truest beauty is on
        the inside
This woman may never be able to give you the world
        but my heart will always race home to you
until the day comes when tomorrow doesn't find me
        but even then you can believe that I still do.

Under Your Spell

Almost since the moment we first met
        you've had be dangling
                breathlessly under your spell
quixotically you've had me tilting at invisible
windmills
        chasing unhappy endings
                to clandestine fairy tales
yet, I always seem to stay
        one hurt away
                from finally being over you
and just one touch away
        from giving myself
                to someone new
but as if you hold the camera to my soul
        you always seem to know
                when to make your presence felt
reacquainting me with the tumultuous resurgence
        of your thunderous passion
                knowing it will make my resistance melt
usufructary you command
        both my body and mind to be drawn
                back into the bleakness that is us
and once again I'm left dangling
        breathlessly under your spell
                a victim of my intemperate lust

Strength To Speak

Why do I feel the need to tell you things
        I thought that you would prefer not to know
is it because I've lived to much of my life
        hidden inside some kind of self imposed
        escrow
Never allowing your love to prove
        whether it's strong enough to hole the truth
instead, I have portrayed the reckless renegade
        chasing my misspent youth
Only occasionally eluding to the person
        it's taken me so much heartache to become
disguising my tears and emotional battle scars
        behind the artistry of a poetic sun
Finally I've come to the realization
        that when the truth goes unspoken it's the
        same as telling lies
and to many people that I love
        never got to know me before our final good-
        byes
Because I didn't have the courage
        to no longer side step and not pretend
but, now from a healthy place in my life
        I'm happy to introduce myself as an out lesbian
This is about far more than women
        with whom I've enjoyed the felicity of their bed
because if I never make love to another woman
        I'd still be a lesbian just underfed
More important are the women who have touched
my heart

and those that have selflessly nurtured me
cradled my insecurities, forgave my distractions
        and encouraged me to seek the person I was
        afraid to be
It's from the tapestry of these women's courage
        that I have woven the strength to speak
in hopes that our love will be another blow
        to the myth of homosexuality's defeat.

She

She prances delicately around in my mind
touching and tempting every nuance of my being
her very essence beguiling, tantalizing daring my
senses not to respond the mere thought of her
She enchants my creativity with the flirtatious
sonorous motion of her body as she moves slowly
away from me
intoxicating me with her alluring lusty scent that
lingers behind prancing invitingly
in the air reminding me of the soft sensuous music of
the dulcimer
opening my mind to all the vibrant possibilities that
are her
miserly I've treasured every unencumbered moment
that she filled my thoughts and captured my attention
like no other
haggardly I waited and wanted her to sweep her long
flowing hair away from her beautiful face and allow
me to see
to finally and forever know
that she is you
this woman who holds my heart and owes my
dreams is you
you, who's love I knew for a tender moment
before you slipped fluidly through my fingers
and longingly into my heart.
She is you.

And I Miss You

You saw me, I saw you
and neither of us knew what to do
so we turned to walk away
as if there was nothing left to say
just like strangers passing by
until I read it in your eyes
that you miss me
and I miss you

I knew I loved you once
but I thought that time was gone
until I saw you standing there
and I knew that I was wrong
as my smile started to slip
you could read it on my lips
that I miss you
and you miss me

I reach out to touch your face
and got lost in your embrace
then we both began to cry
for the wasted time we let pass by
we wanted each other so much
we could feel it when we touched
that you miss me
and I miss you

My Angel Lover

Once I laid beside an angel
she showed me the world through her eyes
She taught me how to laugh, how to love
and then she taught me how to cry

My angel snatched my heart from my chest
and balanced it delicately on a ledge
the she dared me to dream, to believe
to have faith enough to step away from the edge

She serenaded me in the warm glow of her magic
touched me in places I didn't even know exist
tamed my doubts and quieted my fears
captured my imagination and guided me to new risks

My angel enriched my senses, enchanted me with her
smile
she gave me the courage to want and the strength to
hope
She gifted me with her gentleness, dazzled me with
her desire
and left me with a shattered heart feeling like a joke

She left without a word of good-bye, no reason given
just a morning smile and a whispered forever
taking with her the best of me
leaving behind the rest of me to revel in our time
together

Sealing off my emotions losing myself in the moment
in too many beds under all the wrong covers
Hoping that they could help me to both remember
and forget
how right it felt to lie beside my angel lover

Once I stop feeling sorry for myself
I knew my life was better for having had her in it
she taught me to give myself totally to love
by laying beside me for an angel's minute.

Caron, Thanks For Penciling Me In

So many times you tried to warn me
     you could hear her footsteps walking on my
     heart
why couldn't I see that she was only
     using my love as she waited on another to start

Every single time she called me
     I took my leave from being loved by you
but you only smiled and promised to be waiting
     when her fun with me was through

You said your dance card was empty
     it was your pleasure to pencil me in
and that if I couldn't keep my promises
     we could start over just being friends

You planned a get away week for us in Toronto
     said it was the perfect city to fall in love
but when she called and invited herself to join us
     you heard me thank the Gods above

When she left me in that restaurant
     wearing her drink upon my face
again you offered me your comfort
     and you tempered my disgrace

You teased me about cupid
     said he mistakenly fired his bow
I love her, you love me
     and neither of us knows how to let go

I want you to know that I know
  it was you that helped my heart to heal
and I'm sorry when it was whole again
   you were disappointed by what I did not feel.

No Love Is Ever Lost

No love is ever lost
        it sometimes seeks delays
                when we say good-bye
                        and go our separate ways

Often we try to hide it
        in the arms of someone new
                but starting over before it's finished
                        is one of the hardest things to do

Somehow the memories always to find us
        whether we want them to or not
                they lead us by the heart
                        over the pain we hoped we had
                        forgot

It's the saddest sound to hear
        the misery of letting go
                the anger, the fear, the sorrow
                        makes the healing come so slow

In every life the sun also rises
        you find the will to live
                in the eyes of a gentle stranger
                        who awakens your need to give

No love is ever lost
        it only gets misplaced
                until she quietly comes along
                        and you see forever in her face

Pieces of a Jigsaw Puzzle

Pieces of a jigsaw puzzle
scattered all around
some of the pieces missing
all the corners torn

Gently you came into my life
and a quiet change begin
in your eyes I saw my future
in your hands I made a friend

Calmly you eased by doubts
and chased away my fears
taught me that some of life's greatest pleasures
are best expressed with tears

Amorously you laid beside me
and helped me reach new heights
seeing things deep inside me
that may never have come to light

Pieces of a jigsaw puzzle
gathered close around
all the corners mended
all the pieces found

Love Revisited

Hey Darling,
here I am again
I'm not the same scared naive girl
that you knew back then
tonight no wasted words
of love need be spoke
life has taught me
hearts really do get broke
tears get cried
and people cheat
times to short
to be discreet
I'm learned so much since that night
when I left you cold and alone on the beach
with Carole King singing and you swearing
heaven was within our reach
I was so worried that it wouldn't be as good
as you envisioned in your dream
but now I've found my passion
and I know, I know how to make it scream
tonight may not be magic
but I'll make it damn good
Amy don't spend the rest of you life
wishing that you could
just take my hand
I'll show you it's not too late
out there beneath the stars
where heaven awaits
come on Darling
here I am again

I'm not the same scared naive girl
that you knew back then
so no wasted words
of love need be spoke
life has taught me
hearts really do get broke
climb aboard Amy
let's finish the ride
I've got the same old blanket
and a little less pride
tonight

There's Nothing

There's nothing quite as sad
as a love that has gone bad
when the time for being together
runs into inclement weather
leaving nothing left to do
but admit it's really through
There's nothing quite as sad!

There's nothing that hurts as much
as a lover who has lost her touch
forgotten all your secret places
calls out the names to different faces
stares at you with that absent look
knowing this is a blow you shouldn't have took
There's nothing that hurts as much!

There's nothing quite like missing you
wishing I was still kissing you
aching to feel you by my side
so just once more I can feel alive
knowing you moved on to someone new
now she's loving you the way I want to do
There's nothing quite like missing you!

There's nothing that chills you more
than to see your heart walking out the door
knowing there is nothing you can say
that will make her want to stay
no tears, no kiss, no last caress
just good-bye and I wish you all the best
There's nothing that chills you more!

Speak Her Name

I seem to always find a way to say no
when I know she needs to hear yes
I give her the worst of me
when I truly want to give her my best
I allow moments to drift between us
without showing her how much her love means
I portrait the stifled business suit
instead of falling into her like a comfortable pair of
old jeans
I fight the part of me
that screams out her name
I wrestle with the soul of me
but she sees it just the same
I hold my heart in check,
but then she touches it and it flys
I look for answers to unasked questions
never brave enough to see them in her eyes
she's that woman I loved long ago
the one I will not meet until tomorrow
she laughs at my weary jokes
embraces my pain and makes me face my sorrow
she grants me access to excess
nothing will ever be the same
yet, I have not found the courage
to finally commit and speak her name

The Dance of Smoke And Im Nuuuu

This morning I was gifted with two souls
dancing vibrantly across my computer screen
speaking haunting words in passing
each wondering what they might mean
both silently wishing by conversation's end
that the words would be softer instead of so tart
while they tried to casually disguise
the hushed tears of a sad and lonely heart
perchance these incidental meetings
are more the strangers sharing the still of night
maybe it is a handwritten invitation from romance
flirtatiously taunting them to share in love's delight
as we the spectators sit quietly
trying desperately not to interfere
even though the shadows of our own heartaches
are the same reasons we are all here
but this morning it is nice to see two souls mingling
perched on the edge of an emotional breakthrough
and we will all walk away a little gentler
for having watched the dance of Smoke and Im
Nuuuu

Good-bye Begins With I Love You

Every time I look into loves eyes
my heart begins to cry
I am reminded that I love you
are the first words of good-bye.

every time she says her love is yours
please know her words aren't true
she is only marking her time
waiting on another love to pass through

Even if it is hidden behind a lacy veil
or a tauntingly seductive smile
know promises of forever
are only offered to beguile

Endings always come, love always leaves
just like the snow that falls from the winter sky
another broken heart must learn
there is nothing good in good-bye

When A Woman Loves A Woman

When a woman loves a woman
she loves her with all that she is worth
she admires her strengths and embraces her
weaknesses
she needs her as a friend, respects her as an adversary
she sees the world in her eyes and forever in her smile
she wants her in her bed, but even more importantly
she want her out of it
she loves when they are together just being them
but she always remembers
that it was her being her that first caught her attention
When a woman loves a woman
she finds all that she is capable of being
and then she finds a way to be more.
In the quiet of that love she learns that hers are
indeed the hands
in which this someone can safely place their heart.

My Innocent

She said come lie beside me
come touch my soul
my sweet little innocent
there's so much you need to know
you've been hiding from yourself for far to long
please come play while my light is still strong
as I laid beside her
she kissed both my hands
whispered to me softly
she said don't worry
we will take this real slow
and we won't go any further
than you want us to go
but you've been hiding from yourself for far to long
please come play while my light is still strong
my sweet little innocent
tonight I'll show you the world
and I'll kiss your tears away
when the woman leaves the girl
I'll be as gentle
as you need me to be
just let me be the one
who helps to set you free
because you've been hiding from yourself for far to
long
please come play while my light is still strong

Women With Blonde Hair

My very first lover
had the face of an angel framed by long blonde hair
she scratched her initials so deep in my heart
that I can still feel them burning there

I was her eager pupil
so willing to be taught
only her lessons left me feeling
liked I'd been run over by a juggernaut

The one thing that confuses me
because my feelings are so strong
is that it's dark hair women that interest me
but it's always this vicious blondes that take me home

The lover of my ex-best friend
was born a blue eyed blonde
she had a wicked way of beckoning to me
that stirred my urge to respond

Though she was barely on the right side of twenty
she knew all the secrets to a woman's sin
and when she laid it at my feet
I betrayed my best friend

These women with blonde hair
are going to ride me to my death
every time I think I'm over one
another takes my breath

Linda Hamilton caught my attention

while on television romancing the beast
Melissa Etheridge completely garnered my
imagination
singing her songs with enough passion for a lover's
feast

Now I may have to face the truth
and admit I may have been mistaken
it's not the dark hair beauties that turn me on
but these vicious blondes I have forsaken

Outing Myself

Whispering on the wind tonight
I heard the resounding voice of change
holding me accountable
demanding that I explain.
Why I never took my place in line?
Why I never joined the fight?
Why I've never reached out to hidden lovers
when we are all facing the same plight?
 It accused me of enabling the spread
 of intolerance, bigotry and hate
 by silently walking away
 instead of at least being irate.
 It questioned how I could bask in a woman's love
then introduce her as just a friend
 over shadowing the beauty of our union
 by the darken confinements imprisoned within.
 The voice spoke to me of history
 how change begins with one is not a lark
 and of others who's courage of their convictions
 chose the course on which they embarked
 It convened me to come forth
 my not doing so would be remiss
 so, I proudly add my voice to those will not allow
 our right to love to be dismiss.

West Virginia

I turned twenty-three in West Virginia
with the only black woman I have ever known
she was singing out my feelings at the piano
I bought her a drink and she took me home

She laid me on her bed and said don't worry
I'm going to teach you what no teacher has ever
taught
then she smiled, promised that when I left in the
morning
I'd know things my mother didn't know to warn me
about

When I reached to turn the lights off, she said leave
them
great sex shouldn't be hidden in the dark
besides when I rob you of your virginity
you're going to want to see where the devil burns his
mark

I thought that I should tell her
I'd given mine to a fallen lover a few years ago
only before I could get the words out
she said, don't waste time telling me things I already
know

I was startled when the fullness of her breast sprang
forward
one had a tattoo of a blue rose crying bloody tears
as if she knew what I was thinking, she pressed it my
lips

and said, take the rose's pleasures they will quiet all
your fears

She was right, because before that night was over
I had shouted out my joy in languages I don't even
speak
she trussed me to her bed with endless joy
and dangled my sanity off of reality's peak

When I left her bed that next morning
she asked if it was everything she promised it would
be
I was six weeks out of West Virginia
that woman's touch was still pleasing me.

Loves of a Lifetime (Part 1)

Yesterday I walked around holding hands with all the
loves of my life
some still reach out to me behind the titles angel,
mother, lover, wife
in my youth love was dark and mysterious,
capricious as the night
though I loved from a whole heart I was lost between
the wrong and the right
struggling back and forth running away from the
truth that was me
sacrificing the love I held in the palm of my hands, for
a mirage that would never be
Heather touched me in a time of innocence and
gingerly taught me how to love
occasionally she whispers across by life with
guidance and wisdom from above
Susan sang her songs of love to me across a busy
Indiana street
in stolen hours from her husband arms, Beth taught
me how to cheat
Lisa resounded into my life like the stock markets
opening bell
before our years together were over, we dragged each
other in and out of hell
more than once it was Donna's friendship that
rescued me from that pain
Lori's youthful energy reminded me how good it felt
to play outside in the rain
but it was Caron's love, that stood guard and gave my
heart the time it needed to mend

only when all the healing had taken place, wanderlust sought me out again

One tried to endure, falsely believing that she could use time as her key

only sadly, the truth was the heart that her love can touch would never belong to me

Another offered me friendship but we mistakenly thought it was more

at least now our souls know the answer to what they are so desperately searching for

A love that will bathe me like the warmth of the golden summer's sun

when she thinks we've reached our zenith I'll show her what's to come

today while spending time with each of these ladies I only wished that somehow

I could have been the person then,, that their love has taught me to be now.

Rules, Wishes and Dreams

One touch, my closed heart unfurled
One kiss, changed my view of the world
One wish for a night that never ends
One dream to share this dance again
One chance to rewrite the rules of love
One moment when our hearts fit hand in glove
One time when you showed up at my door
made me feel like I never loved before,

there's someone

there's someone
        who dances through my dreams
there's someone
        that has taught my heart to scream
there's someone
        whose presence feels my life
there's someone
        who has taken away my strife
there's someone
        who is with me everywhere I go
there's someone
        that has taught me all I need to know
there's someone
        whose love is so complete
there's someone
        my heart can't help but repeat
there's someone …
there's someone …
there's someone

girl

girl, I cried when I said goodbye to you
and my heart still has not accepted that we're through
the more I think about us, the more I know it's true
because the best of what I am still lives in you.

girl, my mind still entertains you with design
there's not a touch we ever shared that I can't find
replaying bold and vibrant in my restive mind
wishing that our bodies were forever entwined

girl, I cried when I said hello to someone new
pretending that it's over, though I know what's true
you're still apart of everything I think and feel and do
my heart just keeps repeating she's just not you

girl, there's not much more that I can say
just remember my love for you lives a breath away
it is yours to hold no matter the time of day
because my heart lays dormant like an unwritten
play.

girl, I cried when I said goodbye to you
and my heart still has not accepted that we're through
the more I think about us, the more I know it's true
because the best of what I am still lives in you.

Quiet the Wind

somewhere between being young and getting older
she watched as dust settled on all her forsaken
dreams
they became weighted beneath seasons of indifference
discolored in the frozen waters of desire's vacuous
streams
her heart carried the moment of that emptiness
as love became a faded memory of something she
once knew
she believed the hint of her touch could make
happiness crumble
until the goddess of forever brought her to you
now she comes soaring to life lost in your laughter
you are everything she ever hoped love could be
her heart is ablazed with thoughts of grand passion
ready to share a destiny she was once too afraid to see
though her soul is still troubled by yesterday's
pictures
her heart is open, her love willing to begin
she believes that lying safely beside you
is the haven to harness her fears and quiet the wind

PS: Time Hasn't Found Away to Leave Us Behind

Last night I spent a quiet moment
walking around with yesterday and you
trying desperately not to remember
that part of me that still remains true
only somewhere beating in my heart
buried not as deep as I sometimes wish
your initials are still craved upon my soul
longing to once again be indulged by your kiss
in those moments I am reminded
there is still a tear of us living in my eyes
and I cannot help but wonder
if you too are not also sadden by our goodbye
even though I am no longer stumbling
over things that we left unsaid
my heart has crawled off the floor
and fallen into someone else's bed
yet, there are still certain unspoken truths
that the darkness in me always seems to find
a space to reach back across yesterday and know
time hasn't found away to leave us behind

Thank you for taking your time to walk around in my thoughts. As I said at the beginning, I hope that you have found it a walk worth taking.
The art of love is magnificent, the act of love is humbling but more that anything the being of love is simply everything.

Madison Blue

www.ingramcontent.com/pod-product-compliance
Lightning Source LLC
Chambersburg PA
CBHW051423280526
45785CB00003B/1142